SOLO PLUS

Clarinet

with piano accompaniment

An outstanding collection of twenty-three light classics and folk songs from around the world expertly arranged for the first-time recitalist. With piano accompaniment in printed *and* digitally recorded formats.

Cover photography by Randall Wallace
Arranged and performed by David Pearl

Order No. AM 947452
US International Standard Book Number: 0.8256.1682.4
UK International Standard Book Number: 0.7119.6953.1

Exclusive Distributors:
Music Sales Corporation
257 Park Avenue South, New York, NY 10010 USA
Music Sales Limited
8/9 Frith Street, London W1V 5TZ England
Music Sales Pty. Limited
120 Rothschild Street, Rosebery, Sydney, NSW 2018, Australia

Printed in the United States of America by
Vicks Lithograph and Printing Corporation

Amsco Publications
New York/London/Sydney

Contents

SOLO PLUS

Clarinet

with piano accompaniment

My First Recital

A Frangesa

Costa

Tempo di marcia ♩= 96

A Media Luz

E. Donato

17
22
mf–f
mf–f
26
30
1.
2.
pp

Allemande

Franz Joseph Haydn

Moderato ♩ = 120

Amaryllis

H. Ghys

Allegro moderato ♩ = 96

Arirang

Korean Folk Song

The Beautiful Jasmine

Ancient Chinese Melody

Moderately ♩ = 76

Bourée

Leopold Mozart

El Coqui

Puerto Rican Folk Song

Dubula

Shoot

African Folk Song

Moderately fast ♩ = 132

14
17
21
24
(opt.)

Grand March

from *Aida*

Giuseppe Verdi

Allegro maestoso ♩= 96

19
23
mp
mp
27
f
f
31

The Cowherd's Song

Edvard Grieg

SOLO PLUS

Clarinet

My First Recital

SOLO PLUS

Clarinet

Cover photography by Randall Wallace
Arranged and performed by David Pearl

Order No. AM 947430
US International Standard Book Number: 0.8256.1680.8
UK International Standard Book Number: 0.7119.6951.5

Exclusive Distributors:
Music Sales Corporation
257 Park Avenue South, New York, NY 10010 USA
Music Sales Limited
8/9 Frith Street, London W1V 5TZ England
Music Sales Pty. Limited
120 Rothschild Street, Rosebery, Sydney, NSW 2018, Australia

Printed in the United States of America by
Vicks Lithograph and Printing Corporation

Amsco Publications
New York/London/Sydney

Contents

A Frangesa

Costa

A Media Luz

E. Donato

Allemande

Franz Joseph Haydn

Moderato ♩ = 120

Amaryllis

H. Ghys

Allegro moderato ♩ = 96

Arirang

Korean Folk Song

The Beautiful Jasmine

Ancient Chinese Melody

Bourée

Leopold Mozart

Allegro ♩ = 120

El Coqui

Puerto Rican Folk Song

Moderately ♩. = 48

Dubula

Shoot

African Folk Song

Moderately fast ♩ = 132

Grand March

from *Aida*

Giuseppe Verdi

Allegro maestoso ♩= 96

The Cowherd's Song

Edvard Grieg

Andante con moto ♩. = 54

The Happy Farmer

Robert Schumann

Moderato ♩= 88

Matilda

Jamaican Folk Song

Merry Widow Waltz

Franz Lehár

Harmony Rag

Hal Nichols

Moderato ♩ = 120

Plaisir d'Amour

Giovanni Martini

Allegretto grazioso ♪ = 98

Minuet

from *Violin Concerto K. 219*

Wolfgang Amadeus Mozart

Tempo di minuetto ♩ = 88

Rondo Aragonesa

Allegro ♩ = 138

Enrique Granados

Slovakian Dance Tune

Traditional

Lively ♩ = 104

Song of Kokkiriko

Japanese Folk Song

Moderately slow ♩= 84

Solace

Scott Joplin

Very slow march

Song of the North

Edvard Grieg

Trio

Johann Sebastian Bach

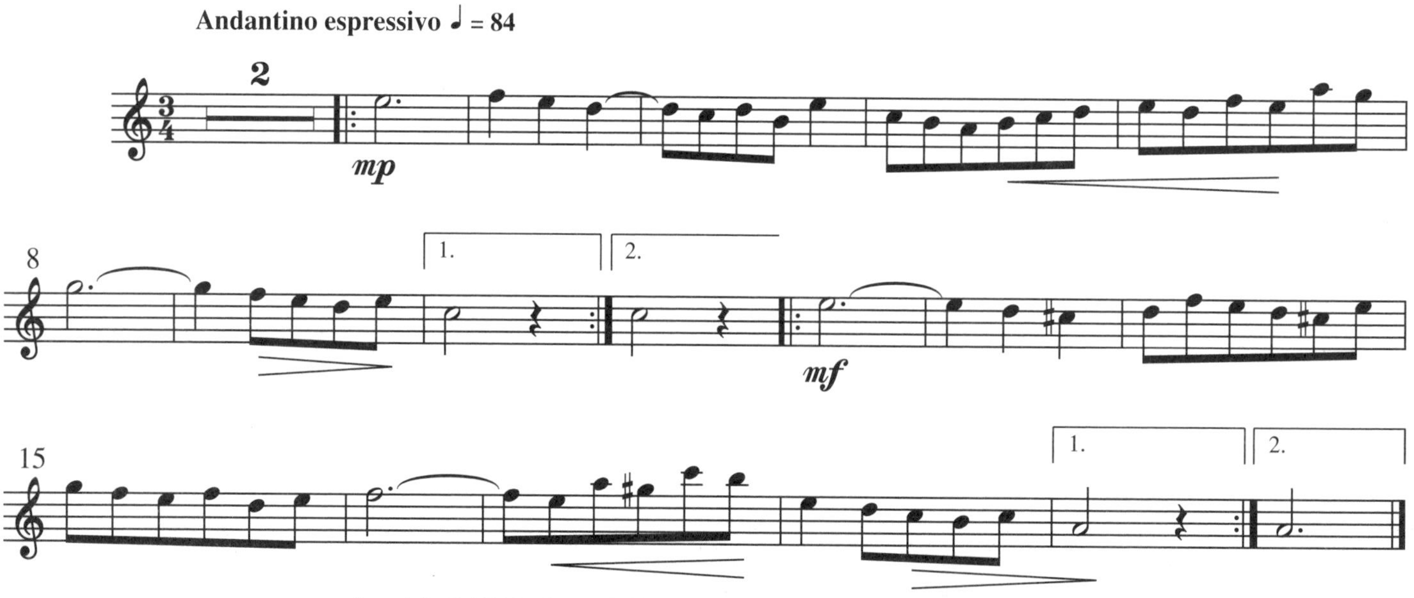

SOLO PLUS

Clarinet

A Frangesa
A Media Luz
Allemande
Amaryllis
Arirang
The Beautiful Jasmine
Bourée
El Coqui
The Cowherd's Song
Dubula (Shoot)
Grand March from *Aida*
The Happy Farmer
Harmony Rag
Matilda
Merry Widow Waltz
Minuet from *Violin Concerto K. 219*
Plaisir d'Amour
Rondo Aragonesa
Slovakian Dance Tune
Solace
Song of Kokkiriko
Song of the North
Trio

The Happy Farmer

Robert Schumann

Matilda

Jamaican Folk Song

Moderately slow calypso 𝅗𝅥 = 69

16
19
f
f
23
26

Merry Widow Waltz

Franz Lehár

Tempo di valse, molto tranquillo 𝅗𝅥. = 60

36
poco mosso
f
f
44
53
61
ff
D.S. al Fine

Harmony Rag

Hal Nichols

Moderato ♩ = 120

19
f
f
24
28
32

Plaisir d'Amour

Giovanni Martini

Allegretto grazioso ♪ = 98

16
f
f
20
mf
p
p
24
mp
mp
28
p

Minuet

from *Violin Concerto K. 219*

Wolfgang Amadeus Mozart

Rondo Aragonesa

Enrique Granados

Allegro ♩ = 138

Slovakian Dance Tune

Traditional

Song of Kokkiriko

Japanese Folk Song

Moderately slow ♩ = 84

Solace

Scott Joplin

Very slow march

19
a tempo
f
f
a tempo
23
27
a tempo
a tempo
31
1.
2.

Song of the North

Edvard Grieg

Trio

Johann Sebastian Bach